Anybody's Game

Kathryn Johnston, the First Girl to Play Little League Baseball

Heather Lang   pictures by Cecilia Puglesi

Albert Whitman & Company
Chicago, Illinois

"Girls don't play baseball," Tom said. "You can't try out for Little League."

"Why not? I'm better than you." Kathryn scowled at her brother. She knew she could throw and catch and clobber the ball better than most boys.

But deep down she knew Tom was right. There were no girls in Little League baseball, and the coaches would never let a girl try out.

It was 1950. Girls jumped rope and played hopscotch. Girls went swimming and played tennis. They wore dresses and helped their moms in the kitchen. Girls did *not* play baseball.

But Kathryn loved everything about baseball—running her fingers along the stitches of the ball, the musty smell of her dad's mitt, the crack of the bat when she hit the ball right on the sweet spot.

Kathryn had been hooked on baseball ever since she was six when she sat on her dad's lap and listened to her first Yankees game.

"And it's going...going...gone!" Her dad imitated announcer Mel Allen.

"Go Yankees!" Kathryn and her dad yelled.

On game nights, she wore her dad's old baseball glove and punched her fist into the soft leather.

"Someday I'm gonna play for the Yankees," she said. "You just wait and see."

"I bet you will, Kit-Kat." Her dad smiled. "I bet you will."

By the time Kathryn was ten, she knew the Yankees players like she knew her favorite comic book characters.

From hit-and-runs to sacrifice bunts, she learned all the baseball tricks and all the rules. By the time she was twelve, there wasn't much about baseball that Kathryn didn't know—except how she was going to play on a real team.

Lots of boys snickered at Kathryn with her baseball glove. But some of the neighborhood boys noticed she had a good arm. They needed more players to get a game going and asked her to join them at the sandlot.

Kathryn stretched her small fingers into her dad's glove. Her family didn't have enough money to buy her a lefty glove, but she didn't care. *Thwack!* She caught the ball, then took off the glove and zipped the ball back with her left hand.

Kathryn dove for grounders like "Scooter" Rizzuto. She slugged the ball like "Joltin' Joe" DiMaggio.

And she slid headfirst.

Kathryn practiced with Tom. She practiced with her dad. She practiced and practiced. By the time she was thirteen her muscles knew what to do before she did.

Every night, she slept
with her mitt, bat, and ball
and dreamed about playing
on a real team.

When Tom announced he'd made the Knights of Columbus Little League team, Kathryn clenched her fists. And when he left for practice, her tears welled up like the roar of the crowd.

"Keep still," her mom said. "I can't braid your hair while you're squirming."

"But it's not fair!"

"Then stop your bellyaching and do something about it," her mom insisted. "I read in the paper they're holding tryouts today for a new Little League team."

Kathryn knew she could have made the Knights of Columbus team—
if she were a boy. And she could make this team too—if she were a boy.

She hated watching from the sidelines.

"Cut off my braids!" Kathryn said.

"What?" Her mom gasped.

"I'm gonna try out—as a boy!"

Her mom found the kitchen scissors in the drawer. She held out Kathryn's braid and paused.

"Go ahead." Kathryn closed her eyes.

Snip. Her mom cut off the first braid.

Snip, snip. She cut off the second.

Kathryn ran to the bathroom and stared in the mirror. Not bad—she sure wouldn't miss those pink bows her mom always made her wear.

Kathryn grabbed her dad's glove and borrowed some pants and a baseball hat from Tom's room. As she tucked her short hair up into her hat, she froze. Oh no! Who ever heard of a boy named Kathryn?

Her mom gave her an idea—an idea that just might work.

Kathryn sped off to the field. Her heart raced faster than the bike pedals. Would the coach believe she was a boy?

At the field, she didn't know any of the boys. What a relief!

As she walked over to the sign-in table, her stomach danced like a knuckleball. She hoped her mom's idea would work. Picking up the pencil, she took a deep breath. Then she signed in as one of her favorite comic book characters: "Tubby" Johnston.

The coach hit fly balls and grounders. When he called out, "Tubby," Kathryn lined up her pop flies perfectly. She shuffled sideways to block ground balls. She scooped up balls, took off her glove, and fired them back. Nothing could get by Tubby Johnston.

In the middle of tryouts, Coach called her over. Had he figured it out?

"Here, try this," Coach said, handing her a lefty glove.

"Thanks, Coach," she said, relieved, and slipped the glove on her right hand.

On the third day of tryouts, Coach put her at first base. Kathryn was small, but she could stretch far and jump high.

No bounce was bad enough for Kathryn to stop. And no throw was too wild.

At the end of tryouts, Coach announced the players who'd made the King's Dairy Little League team.

"Tubby Johnston," he called out. Kathryn had to stop herself from squealing. She was on a real baseball team!

That night she told her dad the news, and he hugged her tight. "That's my boy, Kit-Kat! You will be great out there."

Even Tom was a little impressed.

Playing baseball on a team was heaven, but it was tough pretending to be a boy. Some of the players asked her if her name was really Tubby. Did they know? What would happen if Coach found out?

All the worrying was taking the fun out of baseball.

One day at practice she got up her nerve. "You've gotta know something, Coach," she said. "I'm a girl."

Coach was quiet.

Maybe he was thinking about what the boys would say or what the other teams might think.

Maybe he was thinking about kicking her off the team.

"You know," he said, "you're a darn good player. And we need you at first base."

When the team found out, they didn't care either.
They cared more about winning.

Every night, Kathryn admired her uniform and counted down the hours until her first game.

At last, on June 19th, 1950, the King's Dairy team took the field for the first time. Kathryn hustled out to first base. Some people in the stands booed her. Word had spread about "Tubby" Johnston.

She pretended not to hear them. She'd show them that girls *can* play baseball.

Kathryn stretched...and jumped...and dove for balls.

A reporter praised her fielding and wrote that "she can hold her own with other male members of the team." Kathryn wished she'd had a chance to clobber the ball, but the pitcher walked her three times.

The King's Dairy team came out on top that day and went on to win lots of games.

The next season, Little League Baseball would create a new rule saying, "Girls are not eligible under any conditions." For more than twenty years, girls would struggle and fight to play the game they loved.

But for one summer in 1950, Kathryn Johnston played first base, batted third, hit home runs, stole bases, and slid headfirst. Many people crowded the stands to watch a girl play Little League baseball...

Yankee Stadium, September 27, 2006

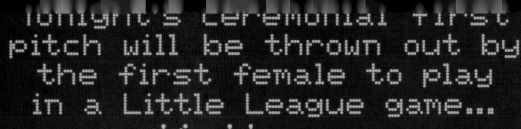

Tonight's ceremonial first
pitch will be thrown out by
the first female to play
in a Little League game...
Kathryn
Johnston Massar

...a girl who never gave up
on her baseball dreams.

Author's Note

When I was a little girl playing baseball and softball with my own brother and father, I took for granted all the opportunities available to me. Like Kathryn "Tubby" Johnston, I was obsessed with the Yankees. I practiced pitching constantly—my dad had the bruised knees to prove it. It never crossed my mind that there was a time when girls weren't welcome on the ball field. What would it have been like to be 13-year-old Kathryn Johnston and be told that I couldn't play the game that I loved? Back in 1950, many local leagues had their own rules. They were flexible about age, for example, which made the inflexibility about gender even more striking. Kathryn was lucky to find a coach who valued talent above all else.

We don't know for certain that Tubby Johnston was the reason for the 1951 rule banning girls from Little League baseball, but it is likely she contributed, and many refer to the rule as "the Tubby Rule." While Kathryn's baseball career was short-lived, in 1951 she was recruited to play softball for the Coca-Cola women's team. At age 14, she was one of the youngest players on the team, which included women in their 20s.

Kathryn wasn't the only girl with a passion for baseball. Starting in the late 1950s, many girls struggled for the right to play Little League baseball. People argued that baseball was a contact sport, too rough for girls, and that girls were physically inferior.

The controversy finally came to the fore-front in 1972, when Maria Pepe pitched three games for her Little League baseball team. Little League Headquarters issued its standard response and threatened to take away the team's charter if they kept her on the team. Maria had no choice but to leave the team. The National Organization for Women sued Little League Baseball on Maria's behalf, arguing that they were discriminating on the basis of Maria's sex. This created a frenzy of protests. Meanwhile, around the country, about twenty other girls were suing Little League for the right to play.

In 1974, twenty-four years after Kathryn Johnston snuck onto a team, the New Jersey Superior Court ruled that girls in New Jersey must be allowed to play Little League baseball. Most teams responded by suspending their seasons. That year Little League changed its rules to include girls and also created a softball league for girls. Thanks to girls like Kathryn Johnston and Maria Pepe, thousands of girls currently play Little League baseball and softball.

Kathryn's story is exhibited in the National Baseball Hall of Fame Museum and the Little League Museum. Little League recognized Kathryn's contribution by inviting her to throw out the ceremonial first pitch at the 2001 and 2014 Little League Baseball World Series.

In 2006, at the age of seventy, Kathryn finally got her chance to play with the Yankees—she threw out the first pitch to Jorge Posada. And at eighty years old she said to me, "I am beginning to think that because of my advanced age the Yankees are not going to call me up. But perhaps I'll get the opportunity to throw out another pitch in their new stadium." I'm betting she will!

1950

Timeline: Women and Girls in Baseball

1866: Vassar College fields the first organized women's US baseball teams.

1928: Lizzie Murphy becomes the first woman to play for a major league team in an exhibition game.

1931: Jackie Mitchell, playing for the Chattanooga Lookouts, strikes out Babe Ruth and Lou Gehrig in an exhibition game. The Commissioner of Baseball then voids her contract.

1943: The All-American Girls Professional Baseball League (AAGPBL) is founded to keep baseball alive during World War II. More than six hundred women play in the league over its twelve seasons.

1946: Edith Houghton becomes the first woman to work as an independent scout in Major League Baseball.

1950: Kathryn Johnston is the first girl to play Little League baseball.

1951: Little League bans girls from their teams saying, "Girls are not eligible under any conditions."

1952: Major League Baseball bans teams from signing contracts with women.

1953: Toni Stone becomes the first woman to play in the Negro American League.

1974: Girls win the right to play Little League baseball.